Religions Around the World

Christianity

Anita Ganeri

raintree
a Capstone company — publishers for children

Raintree is an imprint of Capstone Global Library Limited, a company incorporated in England and Wales having its registered office at 264 Banbury Road, Oxford, OX2 7DY – Registered company number: 6695582

www.raintree.co.uk
myorders@raintree.co.uk

Edited by Linda Staniford
Designed by Jenny Bergstrom
Picture research by Pam Mitsakos
Production by Steve Walker
Originated by Capstone Global Library
Printed and bound in China

ISBN 978 1 4747 4217 7
21 20 19 18 17
10 9 8 7 6 5 4 3 2 1

British Library Cataloguing in Publication Data
A full catalogue record for this book is available from the British Library.

Acknowledgements
We would like to thank the following for permission to reproduce photographs: Alamy: Alex Segre, 26, Bob Daemmrich, 23, LondonPhotos/Homer Sykes, 20, LOOK Die Bildagentur der Fotografen GmbH, 28, nik wheeler, 25; iStockphoto: Andrew_Howe, 19, FatCamera, 15, isitsharp, 24; Shutterstock: aaabbbccc, 9, Alena Haurylik, 29, Art Konovalov, 7, Attila Jandi, 8, AVA Bitter, cover middle, 1 middle, Blend Images, 14, Damon Yancy, 17, Freedom Studio, 16, Lanbo, 12, Mykola Komarovskyy, 21, Pack-Shot, 27, Pawel Kowalczyk, 11, Philip Chidell, 10, Rawpixel, 5, Sybille Yates, 13, Taxiro, design element, Victor Lauer, 4, WitR, 18, Wuttichai Jantarak, 6; Thinkstock: Stockbyte, 22

We would like to thank Reverend Laurence Hillel of the London Inter Faith Centre for his invaluable help in the preparation of this book.

Every effort has been made to contact copyright holders of material reproduced in this book. Any omissions will be rectified in subsequent printings if notice is given to the publisher.

Contents

Some words are shown in bold, **like this.**
You can find out what they mean by
looking in the glossary.

What is Christianity?

Christianity is a religion that began in the **Middle East**. It began around 2,000 years ago. Today, more than 2.4 billion people follow Christianity.

This is the Church of the Nativity in Bethlehem, in the Middle East. Jesus (see pages 6–9) was born in Bethlehem.

Christians go to a church to worship.

People who follow Christianity are called Christians. Christians live all over the world. The United States is the country with the most Christians. Around 30 million Christians live in Britain.

Christian beliefs

Christians believe in God.
They believe that God sent
his son, Jesus, to live on Earth.
Christians call him Jesus Christ.

This stained
glass window
shows Jesus
Christ.

These images
are in a Russian
Orthodox Church.

Christians believe that Jesus came to
save people from their **sins**. He taught
people about God's love for them. He
showed them how to live good lives as
God wishes.

7

Jesus was born in Bethlehem, in the **Middle East.** He began teaching when he was about 30 years old. He went from place to place, teaching and helping people. He formed a band of close followers, called the **disciples**, who travelled with him.

Jesus taught his disciples about God so that they could pass on his teachings to other people.

Many churches have a wooden cross outside, often with an image of Jesus on it. This represents the **Crucifixion**.

After three years, Jesus was **arrested**. He was nailed to a cross and **crucified**. Christians believe that Jesus died and came back to life again three days later.

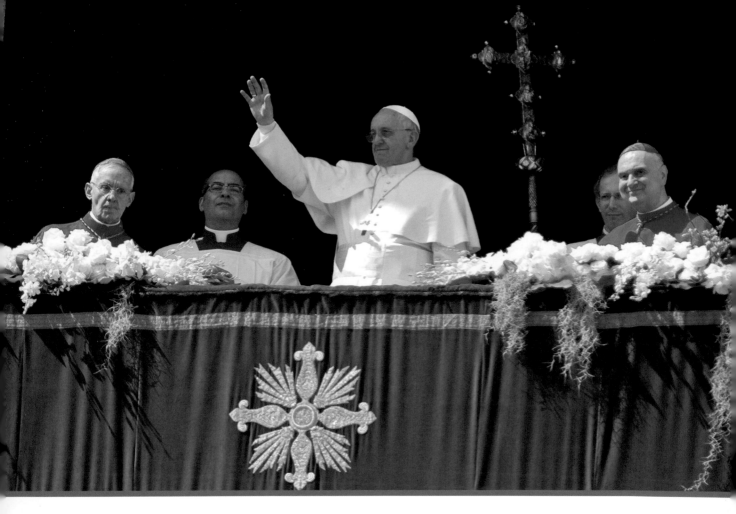

The head of the Roman Catholic Church is the pope.
He lives in Vatican City in Rome, Italy.

There are many different groups of
Christians. They all share the same main
beliefs, but they have different ways
of worshipping. The biggest group are
Roman Catholics.

Another large group are Orthodox Christians. They mostly live in Russia and Greece. In Britain, many Christians belong to a group called Anglicans. They are part of the Church of England.

Cathedrals are large churches. This one is in Canterbury, England.

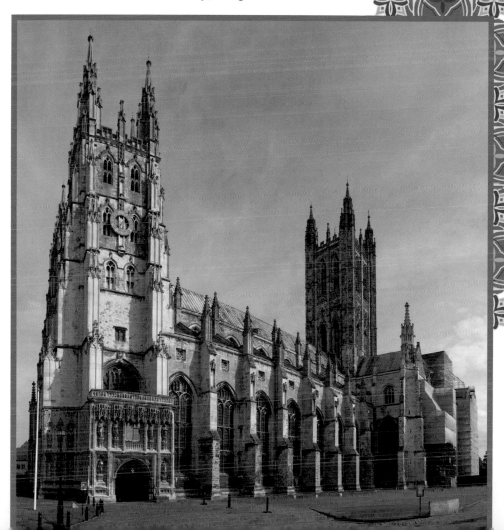

Holy book

The Holy Bible is the holy book of Christianity. The Bible is divided into two parts. The first part is called the Old Testament. It tells about the time before Jesus was born.

The Bible was originally written in ancient languages such as Hebrew and Aramaic.

The second part is called the New Testament. It tells stories about Jesus and the first Christians. It also contains letters and writings by Jesus's disciples and early Christian leaders.

This stained-glass window shows Luke, one of the writers of the Gospels. The Gospels are part of the New Testament.

Christians believe that the Bible is the Word of God. They hear readings from the Bible when they go to worship in a church.

When Christians attend a **service** at a church, the priest gives a talk to help them understand the Bible.

Many Christians also read the Bible at home.

Learning from the Bible is the most important part of worship for many Christians.

Christian worship

Christians have many ways of worshipping God. Saying prayers is a way of talking to God. As Christians pray, they often put their hands together and close their eyes to show **respect**.

Jesus taught his **disciples** how to pray.

Prayers do not
need to be
spoken aloud.

Christians can pray to God anywhere
and at any time. Many people say
private prayers at home. They may ask
God for help or say sorry for things
that they have done wrong.

Christians also go to a church to worship and pray with others. Many churches are built in the shape of a cross. The shape reminds Christians of how Jesus died.

This unusual church is in Ethiopia, Africa. It was built in the shape of a cross.

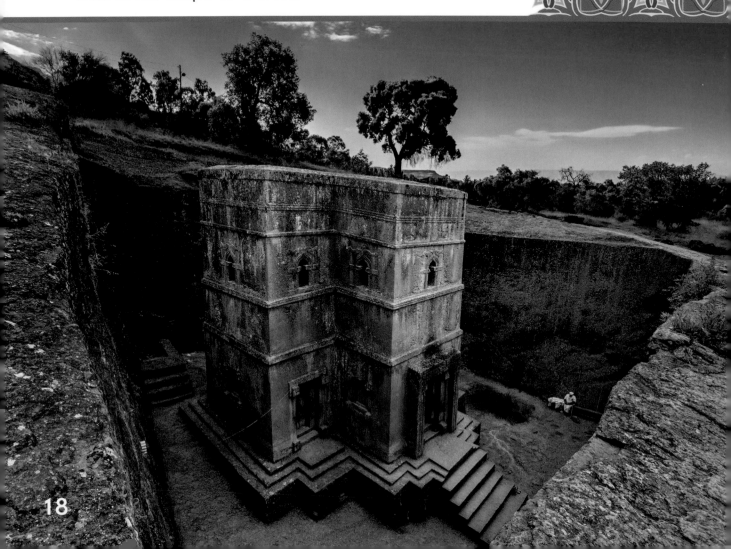

In this church in England, the altar has a cross and candles.

Some churches are very plain inside. Others have lots of decorations. The most important part of many churches is a special table called an **altar** or Communion table. A cross is often placed on it.

Singing hymns is an important part of Sunday services in many Christian churches.

Sunday is a special day for Christians. Many take part in a **service** at church. There are prayers, **hymns,** and readings from the Bible. There is a talk by the **priest** or **minister.**

For many Christians, the most important service is the Eucharist. It is also called Mass or Holy Communion. Christians eat a small piece of bread and drink a little wine. They do this to honour and remember Jesus.

The priest blesses the bread and wine during the Eucharist.

Special times

Many people choose to be **baptised** when they become a Christian. Christian parents often have their babies baptised. The **priest** or **minister** uses **holy water** to make the shape of a cross on the baby's forehead.

Baptism is also called christening, as it is when the baby is given his or her Christian name.

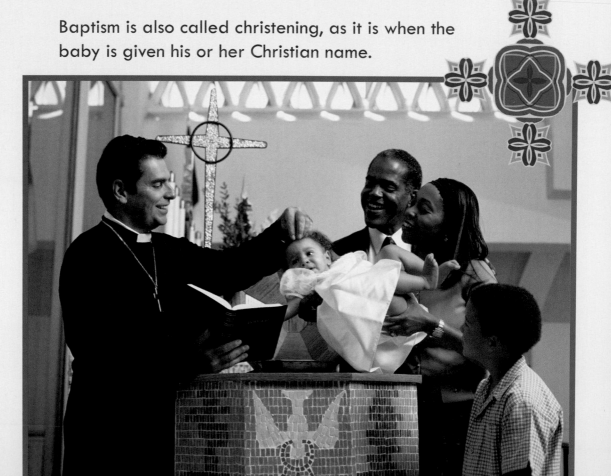

These young people in the USA are taking part in a confirmation ceremony.

Another important ceremony is called confirmation. This is when young people promise to follow their faith and make it stronger.

In a Christian wedding, the bride and groom exchange promises, or vows, to one another.

Many Christians get married in a church. They ask for God's blessing on their marriage. They promise to love and look after each other. They give each other a wedding ring as a sign of their promises to one another.

When a Christian dies, a funeral **service** is held. Prayers are said for the dead person, their family and friends. Christians believe that, when people die, they start a new life with God in heaven.

People often wear black at a funeral as a sign of **respect**.

Christian festivals

One of the most important festivals in the Christian year is Christmas. At Christmas, Christians celebrate the birth of Jesus in Bethlehem, more than 2,000 years ago.

These children are taking part in a Christingle service at Christmas in Westminster Abbey, London. The Christingles represent Jesus as the "Light of the World".

Many churches have a **nativity** scene during Christmas. These scenes use models of the characters from the story of Jesus's birth.

At Christmas Christians thank God for sending Jesus to the world. They listen to the story of Jesus's birth from the Bible. They sing songs about his birth, called **carols**.

For Christians, Easter is the most important time of the year. On Good Friday, Christians remember how Jesus died (see page 9). They believe that Jesus gave up his life so that everyone would be forgiven for their **sins**. This showed God's love for the world.

In Orthodox churches, the Easter **service** often takes place by candlelight.

Easter eggs are symbols of the Resurrection.
They represent new life.

On Easter Sunday, Christians
believe, Jesus came back to life. This
is called the Resurrection. They go to
church to thank God for Jesus's life.

Glossary

altar table in a place of worship, used for religious ceremonies

arrest stop and hold someone by the power of law

baptise pour water on someone's head or bathe them in water, as a sign that they have become a Christian

carol joyful song, especially one that is sung at Christmas

crucified killed by nailing to a cross

Crucifixion when Jesus was killed by being nailed to a cross

disciple someone who follows the teachings of a leader

holy water water that has been blessed by a priest so that it can be used for baptising

hymn song praising God

Middle East part of Africa and Asia that includes Egypt, Iran, Iraq, Israel, Saudi Arabia, Syria and Turkey

minister member of the Christian church who leads services and performs ceremonies

nativity story of Jesus' birth

priest person who leads services and performs ceremonies, usually in a Catholic church

respect feeling of admiration or high regard

service ceremony of religious worship, often in a church

sin act that goes against moral or religious laws

Find out more

Books

Celebrating Christian Festivals (Celebration Days),
Nick Hunter (Raintree, 2015)

Christian Festivals (A Year of Festivals), Honor Head
(Wayland, 2012)

Happy Easter: The Festival of New Life (Let's Celebrate),
Joyce Bentley (Wayland, 2016)

Websites

www.bbc.co.uk/schools/religion/christianity/
Find out more about Christianity with this
fact-packed website.

www.primaryhomeworkhelp.co.uk/religion/christian.htm
Lots of information about Christianity to help you with
homework projects.

Index